Promise of Dawn

i

LITERATURESLIGHT PUBLISHING

Near collectorate, Pathak Colony,
Jashpur Nagar, Chhattisgarh 496331
www.literatureslight.com

Acknowledgement

Poetry has always provided a safe refuge, a rich, vast, vibrant canvas where my thoughts and emotions take the form of these tiny pulsating, breathing poems.

Promise of Dawn would not have seen the light of day without the unstinting encouragement and support of my daughters Sakshi and Aanchal. Each poem has gone through strict scrutiny by the girls, brutal, candid feedback given to modify the content and structure. They have been very generous with the praise too, their words of appreciation mean a lot.

My friends Rumjhum, Persis and Lisha have been the wind beneath my wings, reading each poem and motivating me to pen my emotions with confidence.

My heartfelt gratitude to you too, my reader for having picked up this book, I hope my poems appeal to you. Savour the diverse themes I have dabbled with, I hope some of them resonate with you.

Contents

"Poetry is just the evidence of life. If your life is burning well, poetry is just the ash."

- Leonard Cohen

*"Painting is poetry that is seen rather than felt, and poetry is
painting that is felt rather than seen."*

- Leonardo da Vinci

Promise of Dawn

You carefully fling two tiny fishing hooks
Bait ecstatic dreams out from closed lids.

You then toss the lasso, tow away the moon
Velvety darkness enters my star studded sky.

Your thoughts stealthily creep into my mind
Ensconced in surreptitious glow and warmth.

Pour true love, sheer joy and contentment
In my heart, every throbbing cell of mine.

I spot molten gold hues at the distant horizon
Your soft smile heralds the promise of dawn.

Ode to Mom

Deep rooted, unshakable, branched canopy, smiling wide
Old gulmohar shrouded in a scarlet cover blazing bright
'We're busy and tired' my siblings and I would whine
'Get the clothes in', we had no option but to toe the line!

Tearing them quickly, salvaging them from the summer rain
'They are safe, we're off to play', we would stake our claim!
Petrified, submissive, of her wrath we were mortally afraid
She would massage my hair with oil and tie it in a tight braid

'No shortcuts, keep stirring till you get the perfect golden shade'
Workaholic, fastidious, bulldozed, till the beds were neatly made
Battleaxe, queen of the bastion, our 'Mother Hitler' to the core
Lip smacking food, spicy, sizzling with pungent tempering galore

Slogged, slaved but had no time to spare for even a quick hug
Her pain, disappointments, she ignores with an indifferent shrug
Not one to kowtow to life's challenges, hardy, a woman of steel
Boldly locking horns with Goliath, her latent traits emerge, reveal

Slogs incessantly till the house is sparkling, not even an iota of dust
Fries signature savories, delicious, crunchy, with golden crisp crust
Her day full of chores from the crack of dawn to endless late hours
Cleaning, cooking, adorning 'Krishna'' with fresh, fragrant flowers

No time for drama, frills or fuss, to us she never said, 'I love you''
Our bottomless well of solace, strength, from which we all drew
Mend broken buttons, iron uniforms, huge pickle jars gently shake
Multi task the chores, seamlessly without any respite or a break

Sent us for exams with the quintessential charm of sugar and curd
Any suggestions to hire help; she'd nonchalantly shrug off as absurd
Sunday lunch, 'Sooji halwa' and delicacies like Sindhi "Dal pakwan'
Triangular bliss 'samosas', spicy snacks created with
flourish and élan

Through thick and thin, sunshine and, rain weathered many a season
Stood firm like a rock, took life head on, loyalty, betrayal and treason
Even at 82, still cooking up a storm, roasting, grinding aromatic spice
Our Gulmohar tree, our Mom, our savior, guardian angel in disguise!

Synaesthesia

Love turns my

world on

its head.

I hear whiffs

of your

fragrance.

I smell your

light, lilting

voice.

I see your

soft, warm

breath.

I feel your

shy, furtive

glance.

I taste the

colours of

a smile.

I touch your

pulsating

heartbeat.

Synesthesia

of all my

senses.

Glass Bangles

Shops display vibrant glass bangles, glinting in the sun
Merchants of dreams, promises of merriment and fun.
Lured by the resplendent hues of green, gold and red
Tiny golden specks atop, spectrum of sunshine spread
Delicate transparent colours, breezy, wind-chimy tinkle
Gentle jingling, each move, affectionate vibes sprinkle.

Armful of glinty garish, delicate, fragile bangles reflects
A prism, magic rays of contentment and mirth deflects.
Bale, valayat, bangdi, chudiya, call them what you will
Fills lives of mothers, brides, teenagers, babies, with thrill
Unfolding romance, soft sounds, neither harsh nor shrill.
Scented, fragrant oil to gently, deftly slide on the wrists
Constant companions all through life's turns and twists.

Seeping feminine emotions, colourful circular wonders
Adorn slender wrists, come rain, sunshine or thunder!
Circular dream catchers, undisclosed, unspoken desires
With fortitude bear the stringent test of life's raging fires.

Blank canvas of life infused with tinkling vibrant shades

Milestones etched in golden tints, memories never fade.

Tender, gentle nuzzle, graze, caress on her dainty hands

Abiding reminder of her beloved in faraway, distant lands!

Vows in Henna

Aesthetic rustic designs
floral, geometric enshrine
secret vows and promises.
Unsaid yet eternally abiding
on beautiful feet and ankles
that are constantly grounded.

Tiny tinkling anklets intimately
embrace these divine vows,
seductive as she steps with grace.
With time the promise in henna fades
slowly disappears from her skin
binding them forever, as soul mates!

Wise Potter

Tiny pots and lamps
some piggy banks too
terracotta dust on feet.

Wise old hands coaxing
clay to metamorphose
into bright magical lamps.

Curvy pots that bedazzle
our homes with warmth
and ignite his tiny hearth.

With pride in beady eyes
he looks at his creation
little one waits patiently.

Let's go back to our roots
fill our lamps with oil, wicks
aglow with flickering flames

Eternal Glow

Turning away left, shot off like a broken arrow
In his wake left a dingy, dark deluge of sorrow
Even now thoughts, memories freely cascade
Like an incessant meandering, mountain stream
Rushes gleefully, to surrender, smudge and fade
Merge, meld, emerge with a resplendent gleam.

Magic moments, sealed with stolen kisses, stealth
Wispy dreams woven, our treasure and wealth
Creating poems sans words, portraits sans paint
Fickle fate tied us together in a knot so quaint
As dry leaves from old barks, flutter and break
Tender dew drops gently from boughs shake.

Softly embraced by memory's fragrance fragile
Freezing time, ecstasy, way beyond the tactile
Divine dancing dervishes' as warm breath flows
Pulsating ephemeral body, eternal souls glow!

Invictus
(unconquerable)

A deep new breath in
fills me with warmth,
hollers up the weepy,
whiny thoughts and
gives them a dressing
down, sweeps them out
from tiny cracks in my
mind, piles them up in
a dust picker of smiles!

While they wobble and
make an attempt to slip,
some hold on to the vine
of sorrows, a huge rush of
a breath out, uproots the
vine from which they grew!

Another new breath in
and now my mind just
zings, tiny electrical
impulses imbue me
with a surge of bright
and beautiful thoughts!

*My lens changes, victim
no more, gently dust the
bruises, carry my scars
with pride, armed with
resolve and resilience
combat the Goliaths of life!*

Caramelized Dreams

With flamboyant flourish, sleight of hand
The puppeteer unfolds a show so grand,
Every tiny speck, every intricate detail
Mesmerizes, spell binds all without fail!

Magical realm bedazzled, glittery tassels
Bewitch, beguile into capricious castles,
Ivory towers mislead to optical illusions
Brazen, blatant, resplendent profusion!

Cacophony of raucous glitz and glamour
Divine whispers drowned in din, clamour,
Skirmish, scramble to join the manic chase
Led astray, fumble, flounder in the maze!

Crescendo shatters caramelised dreams
Unscrambles patterns, sets free, redeems,
Elysian kaleidoscope churns dainty designs
A glimpse of the glorious, regal and sublime!

Decadent Wishes

I wish to bask forever and ever
in those deep cinnamon eyes
addictive, like the exotic spice.

I wish to stay still, not even blink
suspend my half breaths within
savour these decadent flavours
in the wildly pulsating ribcage.

Lend me your luscious smile
marinated in your adulation
to bask in loving indulgence
in this cycles- of- life after life.

Beastly Race

The dice of events spins again
Scheming and plotting games begin!
Elbow and jostle to get to the top
Clawing and grabbing till you drop.

No time to pause and breathe
To prey and devour is their creed.
Caught in the incessant beastly race
Fuelled by avarice, pick up the pace.

No room for honour, dignity or grace
Ignoble tricks expended to win the race.
Bruising and squashing, bereft of ethics
Propelled by this heady, intoxicating mix.

The deserving percolated to the bottom
Hedonists float freely to the top scum.
Crouching to pounce, heinous beasts of prey
Sharpen claws, surreptitiously join the foray.
Gorging on carcass, ravaging night and day!

Oblivious of the purpose lofty and sublime
Basal beastly instincts epitomise and enshrine!

Benaras

I need not take a pilgrimage
I close my eyes and there you are!

A million bells tinkle in the breeze
Heady sandal and rose incense.

Conch abuzz with ocean's secrets
Soft, choral chanting of mantras.

Massive oscillating metal oil lamps
Ghats with multitude of devotees.

Floating lamps with flickering flames
Like moving constellations on water.

Marigold garlands bobble in ecstasy
The golden orb, the full moon, shining.

Moving silhouettes of colourful boats
Waters absolving a lifetime of sins.

Holy Communion, creator Lord Shiva
Moving pantheon, the holy Ganga.

Celestial Magnificence

Amber effulgent glow warms me to the very core
Tossing the cosmic dice, spinning it once more
Lapping, lilting waves racing to the pristine shore
Sea gulls devour the scrumptious offerings galore!

Tiny boats spritely bobble, heady with delight
Undulating, lurching towards the horizon bright
Stupendous sudden swells suffuse a ghastly fright
Sailors scurry, adjust sails to combat the sea's might!

Our endeavour seems puny, insignificant and feeble
To struggle and thrive in nature's bountiful crucible
Every grain of sand, pebble reveals the message divine
Life is flitting, ephemeral every crushed shell enshrines!

The secret whispers echo from every bud, every leaf
The span is evanescent, our sojourn fleeting and brief
Exult, regale in abundance, and not wallow in futile grief
Time is striding like a skulking surreptitious thief!

Celebrate the cosmic rhythm that fills our days
Shrouded amidst the mist of materialistic haze
Radiating soft, honey dew celestial magnificence
Dispelling darkness, embracing His benevolence!

Celestial Melody

You may take refuge in a cocoon

Seal your soul secure from love.

You may isolate, cordon yourself

Off with music, yet a murmur of

Memory will find a chink in your

Armour, disrupt your rhythm, deftly

Navigate your fiddle to coax gentle

Unheard of celestial, divine melody.

Closed Doors

You do not open the closed door
despite my constant hard knocks.

My heart's devotion is relentless,
persistent desire to be with you.

I won't quit, patiently persevere
to surmount Your doors and walls.

Intoxicating fragrance of flowers
wafts across permeating barriers.

Drops from the moist soil seep
stealthily through to the new buds.

Sharp beams of sun infiltrate your
guarded fortress through cracks.

Stubborn wind blows over the door
smothers You in a warm embrace.

The traitor notes of Celestial music
escape through the door, reach me.

The Divine vines across Your door
betray, reflecting You in every leaf.

Like the sun rays, fragrance, wind,
water I too will forge my way to You.

Cornucopia of Abundance

Tepid sun penetrates tree shrine
Fill sour mangoes with sunshine
Rain water becomes its systole
Winds bless its juicy golden soul.

Dangling trophies from its boughs
Luscious flavours in each endows
Filling homes and heart with delight
Relish gold goodness in every bite.

Slowly changing sour into sweet
Secret wand divine and discreet
His grace, nothing remains same
Hope, faith transforms life's game.

Children love mangoes, rich pulp
Ecstatic with every delicious gulp
Magic, miracle of such magnitude
Fills hearts with abundant gratitude.

Crescent Moon

Tender silvery glow of the crescent moon

Highlights the tall swaying tree tops with

Strokes and tints of soothing moonlight

Spinning a tapestry seeped with sequins

Myriads of emotions, unbridled rapture

Deep hidden vales of concealed agony

Endless wait, tiny sand grains gently slide

Harbouring firm faith, merciful Maker's

Masterstrokes of vibrant, verdant hues

In the dull monochromatic tapestry of life.

Dainty Daisy

Tossed away to wilt
dug my roots in deep
cleaving right through.
Battered, bruised, eke
out a weary existence.

Dainty no more, resilient
incisive and determined
surmounting challenges.
Firmly holding my ground
smile, hold my head high.

Adapt, adroitly sway with
unforgiving, fencing winds
shredding my core with
razor sharp, lethal strokes
while the sun plays referee.

Quenching my thirst with
generous drops of honey
dew, skies scatter at dawn.
Arching, tipping on my toes
kiss the sexy, seductive sun!

I am triumphant, a survivor
not a dainty daisy anymore!

Day of Reckoning

If on the day of reckoning
He asks you about me
tell Him my sweet name.

If He asks for my whereabouts
tell Him I dwell in your abode
amidst the stars and the moon.

If it is winter in your abode
trace my name with your
fingers on the pristine snow.

If it is spring in your abode
trace my name with your
fingers on your warm skin.

When l meet you one last time
if the palanquin bearers bring
'Dawn', urge her to tarry a little.

When I meet you one last time
If 'Tomorrow' descends in your
abode, urge Him to gradually
unveil the sun from my forehead.

Tell Him about a love like mine!

Denial

She doesn't need pills
for the pain.
She just needs to
understand it.

She submerges pain
in the fragrance
of flowers.

She doesn't need to
hear that you
love her.

She just needs to
accept that you
don't.

Destiny's Child

He wakes up to a world so bleak
Two square feet to curl and sleep.

Empty stomach, his slumber deep
Sweeps him away from the streets.

Lids closed, takes a quantum leap.
Away from dirt, rotten refuse heap.

Into Neverland, of abundance, plenty
Sumptuous platters that never empty.

Big, colourful balloons defying gravity
Caramel popcorn, colourful confetti.

World's economists have the remedy
Dispel the deep darkness of disparity.

Where pillows are not made of stones
Children are not merely skin and bones.

No one dies of vile disease like hunger
None are victims of pillage and plunder.

Blissful world sans man made maladies
Iridescent, golden childhood memories.

Where a single meal is not a dream
For food children walking on a beam.

Like everything else dreams die too
Wakes, grapples with challenges new.

Unlucky, doomed as destiny's child
On whom Lady Luck never smiled!

Distant Dream

Every robust cell oozing with heartfelt gratitude
Preachers sing their song -our positive attitude.

Life's rudderless, purpose vague, not very clear
Vision hazy, shrouded in uncertainty and fear.

Karma has no menu, you just get your lot served
Melancholy, emptiness, is that what I deserved?

Life gurus spin a yarn, with a furtive glance
Mantra is simple, it's choice, change and chance!

When cruel destiny dealt such a festering hand
My choice? Who chooses a life insipid, bland?

Next Trump card they throw is of taking a chance
Heartbreak! He walked away without a glance!

The Final card left in their oeuvre is change
Left with no chance or choice, what can change?

Deceptive, misleading like a state of art Android
Remain inactive, sans functions, null and void.

Lie inert on a table, forlorn, gathering dust
Tethering into Wi-Fi, data is an absolute must.

So a life line, steady net connection is essential
My life too rots, thick rust erodes my potential.

I have the attitude of gratitude, belief in Grace
But without a lifeline it ebbs to slowly efface.

Deafening silence till you can hear loneliness scream
Heartfelt gratitude remains just a distant dream!

Divine Dichotomy

Infinite distance between us separates and restrains
Souls meet, dissolve, barriers, walls, nothing remains.

When together, absorb your fragrance, repose forsake
Alone, insomniatic, languish, endlessly, wide awake.

Together, exude, extol, and exult in a torrent of joyful tears
Alone, racked by a deluge of dread, distress and fear.

With you time takes on wings, moments seem to flee
Alone, agony, searing torment, torture of third degree.

Under the soft moon, stillness, in divine silence regale
Alone, yearn to converse, complain, spin love's tall tale.

Crescent orb teaches us quietude, deep deliberation
Alone, even full moon agitates, fills us with frustration.

With you, He responds even to silent, satiated sighs
Alone, turns a deaf ear, disregards, ignores my cries.

With you I soar the crest, alone, in furrows fret, pine
The Master puppeteer, tugs, unfolds dichotomy divine!

Elusive Krishna

I can't share your image
but your little calf will do.

In his huge innocent eyes
I see unconditional love.

The tenderness of his new
life echoes in the blush ears.

Just strayed into your home
As did you, deep into my heart.

Left as unexpectedly as he came,
as did you, my elusive Krishna!!

Etched in Memory

How is it that
He's always
in my thoughts?

Even when
I am not
thinking.

Eternal Quest

The wild, raging ocean waves tirelessly attempt
To reach the pearl deep in the heart of the shell.

A drop of the ocean trapped in the shell forever.
Eternal quest, endless attempts, agitate waves.

You are beyond my grasp, can't belong to me
That You exist, Your mere presence is enough.

Ethereal Release

Dismal, dreary, parched soul is famished
Every niche, foothold stealthily vanished
Mercilessly squashed whimper of desire
Eternally snared in this murky quagmire!

Flagellating fervently gasping for a breath
Suffering quietly a slow excruciating death
Desires sublimate like they never did exist
Mired in the temptations unable to resist!

When will this relentless cycle ever cease?
When will the soul find ethereal release?
Constant quest for celestial bliss pervades
Unflinching fathomless faith never fades!

Fate-My Friend

Burst of endless anguish seeping and swirling rapidly through
Unable to fit into this anomalous, antagonistic social milieu.
Baffled by the insurmountable mound of expectations galore
Feel the thread slipping, excruciatingly shredding my very core.

Adrift, falling short of the world's warped measure
Sequestered in a world sans laughter or leisure.
Rolling randomly, dazed as the events recklessly churn
Relentlessly, while I wait anxiously for fickle fate to turn.

My world upside down just once, to start afresh, anew
To bid all harrowing setbacks, dreadful despair adieu!
Fling open the doors of destiny, to enter a world of fantasy
Feel the hues of the rainbow, drench in the deluge of ecstasy.

Come on lady luck, about time you knocked at my door
Yearning eternally for just a sip of life, nothing more
Fill my cup with effervescence, bubbling to the brim
Few moments of frenzied fun, nothing melancholic or grim.

Forfeit

All she wanted was to cherish moments with you
for that she could forfeit her heartbeats.

All she wanted was to secure you in her memory
for that she could forfeit her dreams.

All she wanted was to feel your warm breath
for that she could forfeit every caress.

All she wanted was to gaze into your brown eyes
for that she could forfeit every colour.

All she wanted was to watch your face at leisure
for that she could forfeit every clock.

All she wanted was the sweet melody of your words
for that she could forfeit the finest music.

All she wanted was your fingers entwined with hers
for that she could forfeit the Kohinoor.

All she wanted was one glance filled with emotions
for that she could forfeit all her breaths.

So oblivious, indifferent, you forfeited her instead!

Fragile Shiva

Fragile Shiva

Fragrance infused

Fuchsia heartbeats

Firmament prays

Fills souls with rain

Fuses reverence,

Faith, devotion in

Fuchsia Shivas.

Frangipani

As I wait for my cab under the tree
A lone frangipani twirls to my feet!

Exuberance of fragrance and fragility
Accept your tender gift with humility.

Reminds of your abundance and grace
Often life's challenges unable to face.

Swaying branches, twinkling sun rays
Fear of uncertainty, soft breeze allays.

Koel sings ecstatic, melodious songs
For you, blithe soul yearns and longs!

Futile Dreams

Heard the words
That you never said.
Wove dreams futile
Walked away from
My deepest desire.

Cleaved with pain
Told myself again
Not to voice it aloud
Bury so deep within.

Yesterday's dreams
Irk eyes like smoke
Somewhere in life
Yet not by my side.

Walked away so far
But memories close
In fires long doused
Embers still breathe.

Alone in this torment
You oblivious, content
Lost hazy memories
Flood me with agony.

Heard the words
That you never said
Wove dreams futile
Walked away from
My distant heartbeat.

Healing

I have insulated myself quite well
No dull ache, throbbing any more
The scab not yet fully dry, pulsates
Memories, uninvited, gate crash in
Your face, distant, hazy with time.

Open gallery, browse, see your pic
Trace a finger over the broad nose
Proud glint in your beautiful eyes
We both loved the same person, you.

Your narcissistic love, selfie smiles
Kept you blinkered, self absorbed
Ensconced in warm arms of ego
Moved on, flitting like a moth!

I find solace in the golden sun rays
The wind caresses, salving wounds
Tiny ripples, placate my aching feet
Gay, warbling birds appease my soul!

Comfort, being at peace, acceptance
Eke a living, seeking joyful moments
Count blessings, tidings of gratitude.
Watch stray thoughts drift in and out!

No longer in depths of dark despair
Rhetoric questions asked no more
Neither expectations nor let downs
With time gaping wounds too heal!

Hellish Rebuke

My pristine love,
innermost beat.
Seat of my soul,
my mind's eye!

Pure as sound
of temple bells.
Fragile as wings
of dragonflies.

Seed of love
throbs within.
Secretly fuels
eternal longing.

Don't shred my
delicate wings.
On sharp thorns
of hellish rebuke.

Hiraeth
(Nostalgia of home)

Light years away
my old home
tugging my
heartstrings.

Somewhere
near stars
echoes of
memories.

New buds
remind me
of my beloved
far far away.

Winds bring
sepia breaths
star dust kisses
careless whispers.

Moon beams
tender tethers
raise curtains
unveil my home.

A hiraeth
of my soul
bridges of
belongingness.

Sluggish ennui
seeps through
stirring songs
sung long before.

My old home
in silences
between notes
of your raag.

Whispers of the Wind

Far far away yet so close
winds bring soft memories
drag me to a happy place.
I don't need your consent
to dive deep into your eyes.

Your pictures add colour to
fading contours of memory.
Flooding my mind with what
could have been, what almost
was, what fate stealthily stole.

Home Sweet Home

Home is not a location
It has no coordinates on the GPS
It is not a place where you grew up
It's not a place where friends and family live
It's not the place that is our address
Someone giving me a reason to stay is my home.

Home is the person who makes you feel secure and safe
Home is not something but someone
Who is your anchor, reason to return
Home is someone who loves and appreciates
Home is not a place but a person.

Your warm embrace- home
solace, succour of soft breath
anchored to your soul

Your home stands by you when all hell breaks loose
Someone whose presence gives you tools to combat circumstances
Home can look through the veneer of your smile and ask
what is wrong
Home is a person who stands by you in moments of confusion
Home doesn't answer questions or solve your issues
Home is simply there and doesn't leaves

*Home knows about you your insecurities and fears that keep
you up all night
But they complement you in such a way that you feel better than ever.*

Your moist palms on mine
our lines mix, rearrange, reshape
create out destiny

Home is a person whose touch heals you

They teach you to love again this time it won't hurt

Home is a person whose happiness makes up your own

When I describe what my definition of a home is

others don't understand until they experience it

*and I hope you the reader find someone who defines what your
home is*

so that you will never feel homeless again.

A home with a heartbeat!

Hope

The edifice of my love rests on hope
To the world they may look like ruins
But the mammoth arch floods with light
Shattered windows still secure warmth
Remnants whisper what could've been
Entire being pulsates with endless hope
In this universe, away from time, space
Really don't know when or where or how
Ruins of hope echo, I will meet you again.

Hubris

No denying his talents
do surpass many that I
have ever encountered.

Completely saturated
by his hubris, blindly
runs roughshod on all.

Full of self- admiration
preening his plumage
self-absorbed, proud.

Under the fake garb of
humility, the devil plays
fiddle, enticing to hell.

Indian Farmer

His quiet, deep contentment

pales all accomplishments!

Fruits of his labour are bright

abundantly infusing our lives

with a mosaic of robust hues

Indian zesty, piquant flavours.

Juggernaut

Holy trio of colossal chariots

flaunt faith's riot of colours bold

massive design with neem wood

artists magically, sans nails mould.

Jagannath, Balaram and Subhadra

siblings Divine, huge rotund eyes

All-seeing, All -knowing, Omniscient

bless soil of Puri, dry tears, soft sighs!

Kolam- My painted Prayers

At crack of dawn, I clear the ground
Transform it to a horizontal canvas
Invoke Lakshmi, Goddess of prosperity
Wards off nasty omens and the evil eye.

Tiny white dots arranged in neat arrays
connect the dots deftly with arcs and rays
softly chant a spell on the earthy canvas
geometric, symbolic patterns slowly evolve.

Dry rice flour becomes my humble offering
My threshold now adorned with fresh Kolam
Intricate white patterns, my painted prayer
By dusk flies away, becomes one with dust.

My painted prayer teaches me mute lessons
Life's lost moments, once gone, never return
loved ones separated for ever, never meet
Flowers fade, wither, never to bloom again.

Estranged love, never returns, waiting futile
My painted prayer teaches impermanence
At crack of dawn the exercise begins anew
Faded remnants cleaned, start from scratch.

Tiny white dots, in patterns, designs anew
Connect the dots, short lines, artistic curves
To softly breathe life into my painted prayer.

Koto Player

Mystical, elusive koto player
entwined my silly nilly heart
in magical notes of his koto.

Exotic mesmerising notes from
Japan, Arabian desert, stirring
medley of divine Indian raags.

Vanished like a desert mirage!

Life After Life

Wore my heart on my sleeve
Whispers of sweet nothings
Distance bridged by internet
Vignettes of dull digital lives.

Peek for any updates or pics
Empty screen, nothing at all!
Pine and yearn for tiny crumbs
Fingertips like blazing bazookas
Shooting a barrage of messages
Oh! the anguish of unrequited love!

Tiny crumbs far and few between
Parched heart aches and pines
Oh! How the hungry heart hankers
For one beyond my grasp, reach.

Quivering palette of hesitant hope
Monet's fresh lilies breathe life
Dreamlike hues, iridescent colours
Lively, landscape full of happiness.
Your long silences are messages
Ones I overlook, live in abject denial
My poetry dies, loses rhyme, reason!

How can emptiness weigh down?
What drives this wedge between?
Life after life to be together at last
Sadly this life too, silently slips by
Silages of the unfathomable love,
Your intense, fiery passionate eyes!
My laden heart full with emptiness!

A Love Like Mine

Abundance of love
tree of life groans
under its own weight.

Flavours of love so
tart, zesty, astringent
leavens the weary soul.

I try hard to preserve the
fruits, delay their decay
by pickling them in memory.

Label the jar, A love like mine.

Lotus Feet

*You are my refuge
Not my last resort.*

*My love for you is
Like a hill stream*

*Pristine, persistent
Quiet, continuous.*

*Like musical notes
Flowing with breath*

*Your loving glance
Beacon of firm faith*

*Your nimble fingers
On the hollow flute*

*Effortlessly change
Air to magical music.*

*Metamorphose mere
Existence to thriving.*

Memories

Winds bring your soft kiss

Dust motes of universe deliver

Memory, of my beloved!

Woven Baskets
of Dreams

Empty baskets of woven dreams
Colourful cycles, joyful screams
Concrete pillows, a footpath bed
One blanket stands in good stead
A family that sleeps together, stays
together, sharing a well earned rest.

Motley Memories

Memories of
Storms in your eyes
Silence in your voice
Heaviness in our hearts
Tried to bury them deep
Far from the mind's eye
Deep under the sod.
Grow gnarled appendage
Poetry sees sepia nostalgia
Prose putrefies, grows mildew
Distance between the two
Resting in my fecund heart.

My Krishna

Just a glimpse of your face,
intensely mischievous eyes,
just melts my silly-nilly heart.

Endearing yet exasperating
antics of my very own Krishna.
All of a dither, my heart aflutter.

Miles and miles of distance
cannot keep your thoughts at bay.
I bask in my love for you.

Your subtle acts become my
colossal source of indulgences.
Feel your embrace, miles away.

Nautical Advice

When the favourable winds betray, adjust your sails!
Strange! Since when did slender straws have any sails?
Lacerating long lashes of the tumultuous, tidal waves,
Ruthlessly eroding, till my quiet, quivering faith frays
Uncertain if my firm grip will hold or mercilessly drown
Perish wearing a sparkling, unabated loyalty crown!

New Identity

I am

Nothing but a nebulous blur
Etching my new identity with

Longitudes of His loving glances
Latitudes of His indulging smiles
Equator, garnering my self esteem.

On the tilting axis of my Faith
I recreate my lost halcyon days.

Nuptial Ferris Wheel

Constant gyrations, wheel upward swinging,
Heady spin, churning stomach, ears ringing.
Enough she screamed, stop, let me alight,
Drowned in the din, pale, ashen with fright!

Piquant laughter, deeply loved, entertained,
For such intense trauma she had not bargained.
Unwrapping dreams, love laden eyes had met,
Peals of giggles, tingling thrill of bated breath

Fulfilling promises, integral part of the deal,
With a hot passionate kiss it was sealed.
Soon rose tinted cheeks turned alabaster,
Nothing had prepared her for this disaster.

Dismay, distress, let downs, bitter betrayals,
Melding in the cosmic kiln, a sordid tale.
Shattering hopes, desires of a life sublime
Fervently seize the heinous cog, freeze time!

Ode to Krishna

The eternal spring nurtures our endless love
your bewitching smile intoxicates from above
your silent song like a brook gushes through
quivering like a dry autumn leaf, fervour anew
wanton winds of my worship, deftly lasso you!

frenzy of meeting tangles, meshes up my soul
deep trenches of my heart, your face I behold
I no longer seek you, without or in any shrine
dancing dervishes, twirling, to rhythm divine!

Sequestered physically by an endless trail
I gently breathe in the warm air you exhale
Though obscure, millions of galaxies away
I feel your feathered kisses night and day!

Old Raags

Eventually
It's not vows
not proximity
not the touch
not promises!

It's kind eyes
Unsaid words
New sunsets
Blank verse
Old Raags
Soft smiles
Tenderness
That binds
Two souls
As one.

Penumbra

You may scoff at my love
Not respond to my pleas
But your thoughts are in
Every breath, in and out.

Like loyal, shy shadows
Your thoughts follow me
Nagging mildly at times
Sometimes, smothering.

You disregard my reveille
Give me no cognizance
Bulwarking my prayers
Bar entry to your Grace.

Yet.....

Your abiding thoughts
Persist like penumbra.

Pipe Dream

Metamorphosis, an excruciating, complex game,
Grotesque, hairy, obese, satiated with leafy juice,
Traumatic make over, nothing remains the same,
Filigreed, frail, blithe, couture designed to seduce,
Butterfly's

Quest for nectar, rich, delicious, delicately sweet,
Scoured for flowers, why settle for a dull, drab leaf?
Tender, fragile goblets, her luscious lips would meet,
Futile, tiring, attempts amounted to nothing but grief!

Reconciled to fate, looked for any wild, wispy, bloom,
Abandoned hope for anything pretty, exotic or bright,
Dismayed wondered if life would end in dire doom?
Brief, fleeting span ended with her solo, maiden flight!

Alas-

Celestial ambrosia of delicious lilies, peaches and cream,
Ever elusive mirage, a distorted illusion, a pipe dream!

Raag Sorath

Sunday morning at the gurudwara
soothing strains of Raag Sorath
gently ensconce my bruised soul
centre my distraught thoughts
like rain drops douse red embers.

Sorath's soulful notes assuage grief
like a matriarch, the raag embraces
reinstalling faith in Him and His grace
stillness abounds, I no longer crave
the temporal, mundane and fleeting.

I now take the ringside view, learn to
accept loss, love, failure, success, highs,
and lows with equal measure of gratitude.

Rat Race

*Deafening cacophony continues, raucous, surging din reaches
a crescendo*

*Vicious slander, bitter diatribe, incessant harangue and
diabolical innuendo*

*Claw, crush shoulders to get ahead in the rat race, trample,
squash with gusto*

*Inebriated with ravenous greed to maul, mutilate, rip, rent,
devour, slyly stow,*

*Skirmishers don a stoic visage, shrouding debauchery behind
an ecclesiastic halo!*

Refuge

Tiny sparrows
teach lessons
simple, sublime.

Wake chirping
a grateful tune
seize each day.

Past shadows
or future fears
are just futile.

His hand takes
care of tiny birds
on every branch.

They neither sow
nor reap, not in
barns they gather.

If Heavenly father
feeds them, then
He'll feed us too.

In Him they trust
soar ever so high
wings of gratitude.

In Him they find
the only purpose
to live in the Now.

If we make Him
our only refuge
He'll set us free!

Surrender

Your long silences
like tiny flames
draw me
closer

Rush blindly, futile
urge,singed wings
my surrender
complete.

Rendezvous in My Poetry

I go to a secret hiding place, Khwaja's Dargah
My heavy heart's burden slowly ebbing away
Frenzied foot tapping rhythm of rustic Dholak
Dizzy, inebriated heart twirls, pirouettes, whirls

Whisper your name aloud, my world is aglow
When I see your soft smile, I forget to breathe
When our eyes meet, I leave a poem on your lids
Every time you blink, my words enter your soul

Unfathomable grace, blinding beauty I behold
Your radiance with a million eyes I wish to see
The agony of longing, desire lights up my being
Wounded wings exult, delightful, delirious flight.

Prayers softly whispered with unwritten words
Emotions and gratitude in soulful songs unsung
Tender love, unasked, unfamiliar, unlived in me
Sacred place of prayers, rendezvous, my poetry.

Renegade Musical Notes

Which raag did you practice tonight?

A few notes betrayed, left your city

entered my heart and struck a chord

deep within my soul, flooding me

warm showers of your thoughts.

Sacred Strings

Far, far away, solitary
yet total consonance,
with the unmeasured
trills of sacred strings.

Earnest desert rose
unfurls mystic soul,
burst of bright hues
offer unbridled love.

Saga of The Shell

Walking wearily, trudging through the worldly maze
Going through mundane motions, in a mindless daze.
Combating raging tsunamis, determined not to surrender
To the brute lashing of the relentless waves all asunder.
Grasping at the scattered straws, squelching salty sand
Groping for the crest, ending up with an empty hand.

Was this how the hapless oyster wickedly tossed?
Till the dying ray of hope was mercilessly lost?
Somewhere in the vastness severed from its shell
Lost its identity in a gruesome realm some call hell.

The seductive curves of the shell lay bare the story
The sad saga of life and loss some find quite gory.
Plodding through the furrows, continuing to trudge
With every ounce of grit You are my only judge.

Seven Tiles
(pithu, lagori, sitaulya)

A sharp aim, tower of seven tiles
come crashing down, scatters wide.
A sudden wild frenzy to quickly run
gather, balance, stack them up, tall.
With a faint prayer, scrutinising gaze
hypnotise the wobbling jagged tiles
to stop reeling, unsteadily, swaying,
the anti gravity feat spreads smiles!

Another swift ball, the stack implodes
collective frenzy to salvage all seven,
Team up, many hands steady the stack
odd sizes, nervous hands, loud crash!
A simple, traditional, exhilarating game
preparation for life's many curved balls.
Precariously stacking up our lurching lot
only to see it dither, topple and collapse!
Pick up all pieces, determined not to quit
seven asymmetrical, vilely vacillating tiles,
Sum up our life's dramatic, wistful events.
shattering dreams, failure, loss, heartbreak!

Another curved ball comes hurtling at us
gather, stack, accept defeat with grace.
A simple, traditional game played by all,
it wasn't a game but was life's metaphor!
Tumbling towers of tilting tiles, so steep
subtly teach lessons, poignant, so deep.
Triumph, defeat, pride, shame and fear,
Makes the game of life, precious, dear.

Silences

In his silences,
and
his caustic barbs,
I find the tenderest
of love.

"Poetry is thoughts that breathe, and words that burn"

- Thomas Gray

Synchronicity

Gravitating into your orbit,
feeling the centrifugal pull,
to the innermost shrine of
your pilgrim soul, isn't just
perchance, a coincidence!

Tender lingering fragrance
of your tranquil presence
gently assuages, mitigates
menacing, dark skies of life!

Doubts, insecurities slowly
ebb, hellish whirling vortex
of emotions languidly abates!

Quietude and stillness wipe
the frost of fear from the lens,
to clarify my vision and unfold
the mystery and the magic of
this world. Your loving glance
guides the rudder of my boat,
propelling me to His Abode !

Tether

Drawn to you with
an invisible tether
surge heavenward
Like a tidal wave.

Erratic musical note
set free from strings
somersaults, twirls
in soul's trajectory.

You , oblivious of me
but my heart echoes
Your secret melodies
in perfect harmony !!

The Temple Bell

An old, rustic mountain village, serene temple
Against the dull grey darkness of early dawn
The bells resonate deep within the mountains
Solemn sound awakens villagers from sleep
Ushers in the light, resonates till the horizon.

The ringing urging to dispel pain and agony
Deep resonance empties, opens the heart
Undulating sound fills an ineffable yearning
Painful sweetness, longing fills our very being
Unbinds, unburdens, and rejuvenates weary spirit.

Meditative spaces of the auspicious sounds
Disengages mind from the clutter of thoughts
Virtuous vibes enter, nagging thoughts depart
No longer grappling, mind and soul at peace,
In stillness, silence, magic, miracles find us.

As air is to the birds, stillness is to the soul
Perfumed dawn, Divine sounds of the bells
Delicious to the ear, as nectar to the tongue
If petals had voices, whispers of bliss echo
Joy emanates, breathing becomes a prayer.

Threshold

Stepping on
my heart's
threshold.
I willed my
life to you
beloved.
Loving glance
lights up
my life.
My Earth has
found its sky
in you.
My devotion
my love
is true.
Constantly
pine for
you.
Fragmented
without
you.
Together
we are
one

Woven words

hold me

close.

Longingly

ache for

you.

Lodged deep

inside my

heart.

Securely tied

to heart's

threshold.

Unfinished Poem

Searing pain of yanking your roots ruthlessly

Embedded deep in my heart's recesses

Not all saplings flower to bear fragrant fruit

My heart, gaping, rends like an unfinished poem.

Veils of The Soul

Drapery of darkness
Hides-buds, flowers.

But moonlight unveils
stars and my soul to
the eyes of the Lord!

Any distance, longing
this heart cannot hold.

Salve for soul's sores
draw me into Your fold !

Virtuosity

*Like the dazzling stars
many light-years away,
oblivious of their effect,
you, in your ivory tower
tug my soft heartstrings!*

*I....
get on with life, my petty
existence, nowhere.... in
your scheme of things.*

*I can live with all that.....
go through the motions
but what do I tell my
crazy heart and mind?*

*Every dawn heralds your
thought, nights too, heavy
with your memories,
rooted deep within my soul.*

*Even your violin strings fill
me with envy, steel hearted,
highly strung, yet manage to
capture your rapt adulation.*

Wishing you the very best
as you seek stillness, serenity
in the soulful, stirring melodies
that you coax from your violin.

In another life time, another
earthly sojourn, we will surely
meet, as soul mates, be one!
Patiently, I wait for the grains
of sand to pass the hour glass.

Waiting

To wait and wait slowly cultivating the patience
To loosen the clasp, accept rejection and let go
Garner self worth, rejection doesn't define me!

Learning to hold my ground, not to scuttle free
Digging my heels in deep, not crawl back in bed
Trust in God, face odds with guts and gumption!

See my house of cards collapse and scatter away
Yet not give in to anger, dismay or grow bitter
Not complain, gently suppress pangs of envy!

Have firm faith, what is meant, will come to me
Not to complain, why things are so hard for me
Seek solace in my questions, not fret for answers!

Look patiently for the missing pieces of the puzzle
Knowing my masterpiece is bound to be complete
These challenges chisel, shape me into who I am1

Preparing to eventually receive the best in life
Waiting a blessing, brings out my best version
I learn that I get what I need not what I want!

"Every heart sings a song, incomplete, until another heart whispers back. Those who wish to sing always find a song. At the touch of a lover, everyone becomes a poet."

- Plato

"Poetry and beauty are always making peace. When you read something beautiful you find coexistence; it breaks walls down."

- Mahmoud Darwish

9 788194 127482